Halloween

This book belongs to:

Guess What I Am ?
I Start with an A
I am the season of the
year when October 31st happens
1/26

I am AUTUMN

2/26
Guess What I Am ?
I Start with a B
I hate light and like to fly at night.

I am a BAT

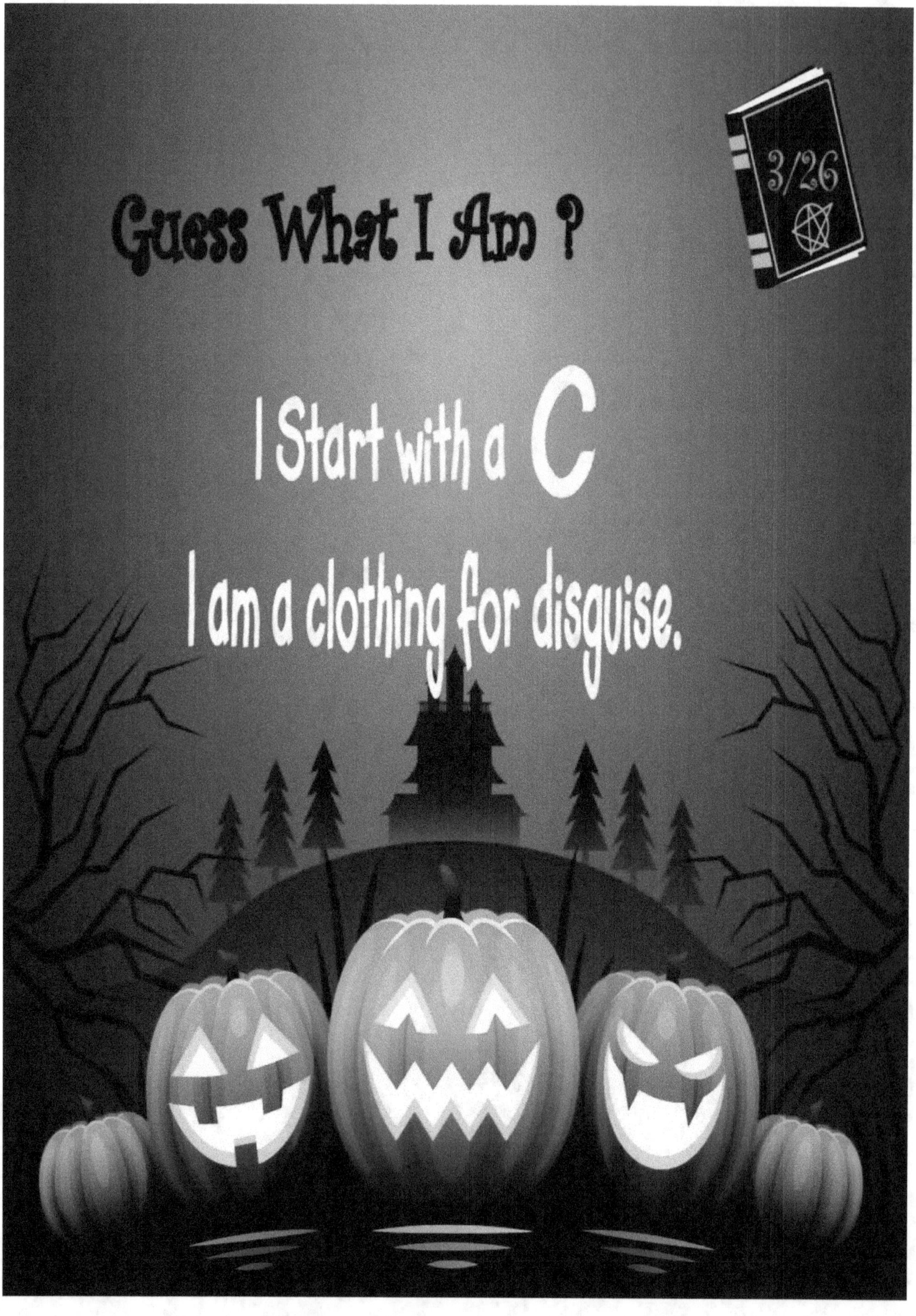
3/26
Guess What I Am ?
I Start with a C
I am a clothing for disguise.

I am a

COSTUME

Guess What I Am ?

I Start with a D
I am the most evil spirit.

I am a DEVIL

Guess What I Am ?

I Start with an E

I am a creature with long pointy ears

I am an ELF

Guess What I Am ?

6/26

I Start with a F
I am a big long teeth.
Vampires often have me.

I am a

FANG

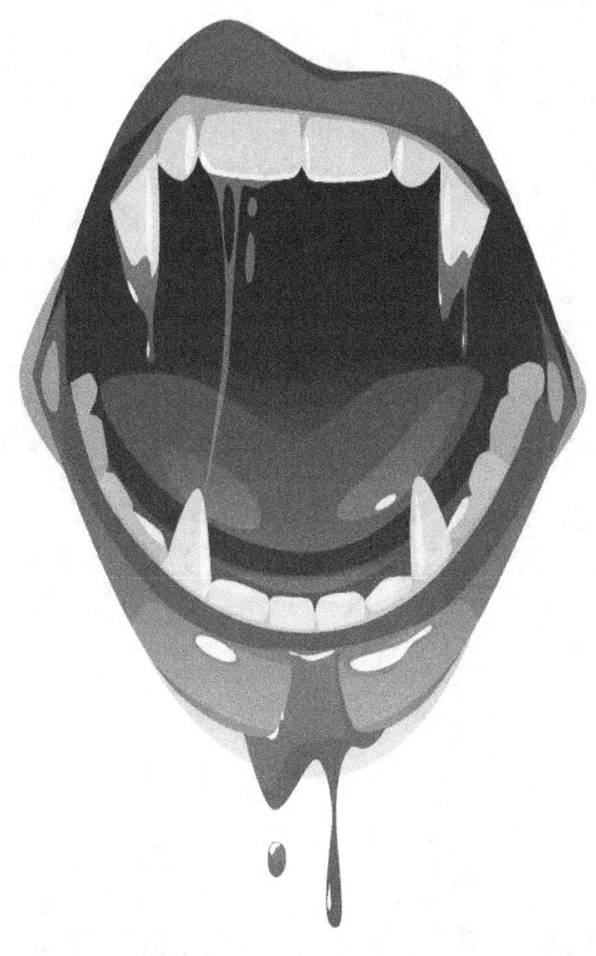

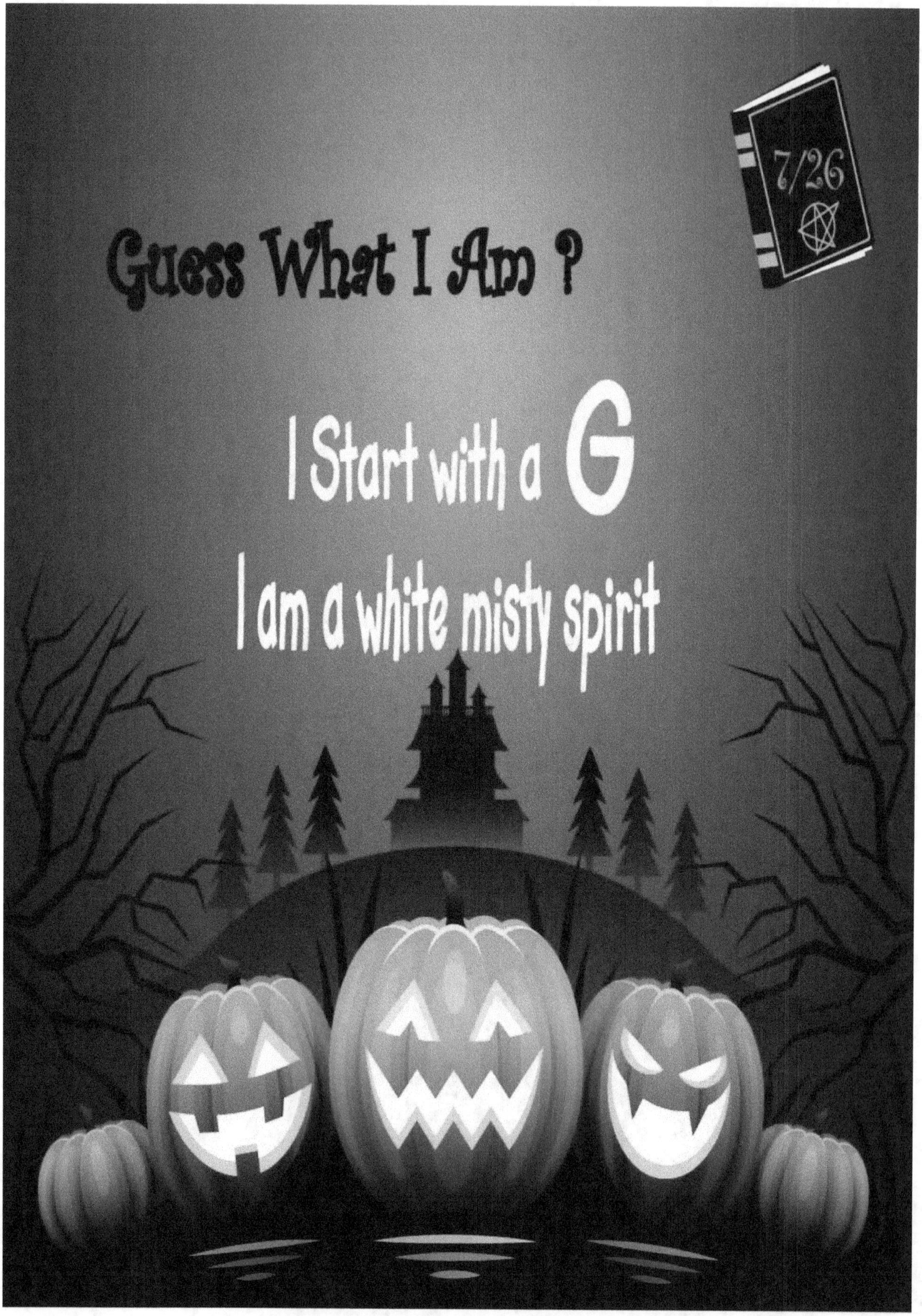
Guess What I Am ?
7/26
I Start with a G
I am a white misty spirit

I am a
GHOST

Guess What I Am ?
8/26
I Start with a H
I am where spirits love to live .

I am a HAUNTED HOUSE

9/26
Guess What I Am ?
I Start with a I
I am what witches chant.

I am an Incantation

Guess What I Am ?
I Start with a J
I am pumpkin's face.
10/26

I am a

Jack-o-lantern

Guess What I Am ?
I Start with a K
I am witches brew pot.
11/26

I am a

KETTLE

Guess What I Am ?

I Start with a **L**
I am a device who gives light by burning oil.

I am a
Lantern

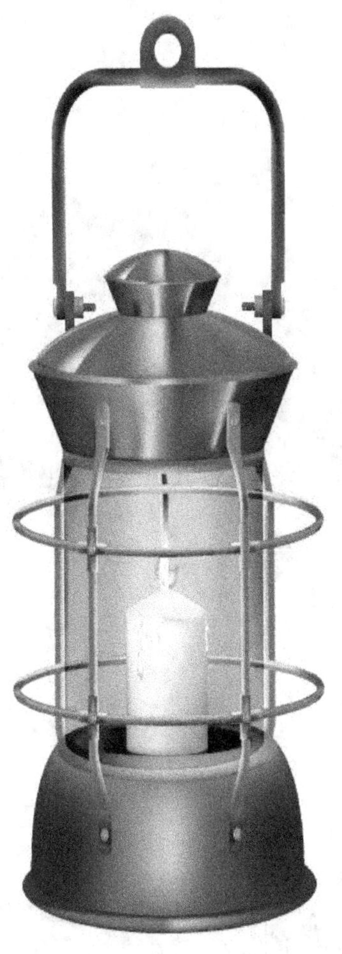

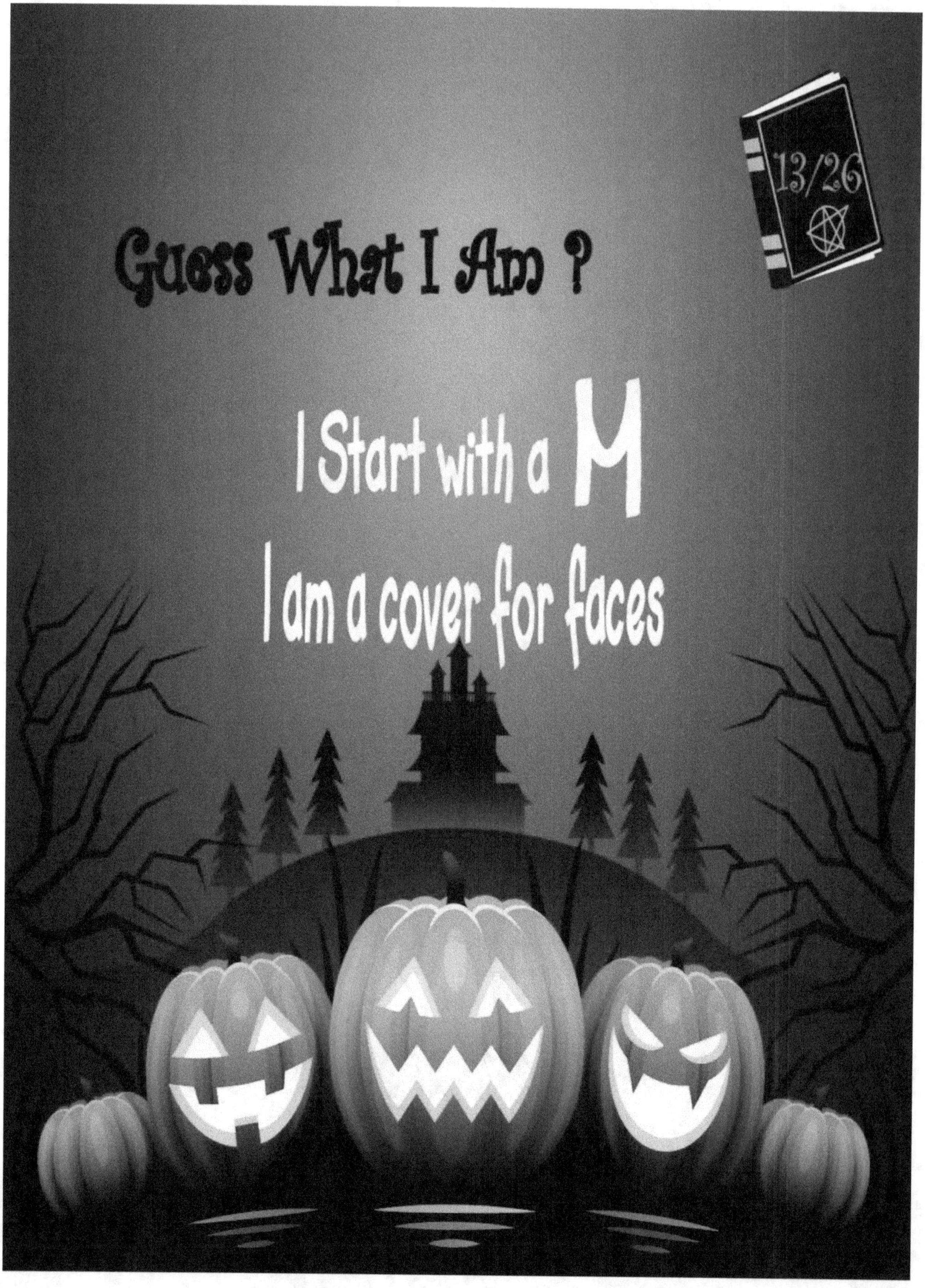
13/26
Guess What I Am ?
I Start with a M
I am a cover for faces

I am a

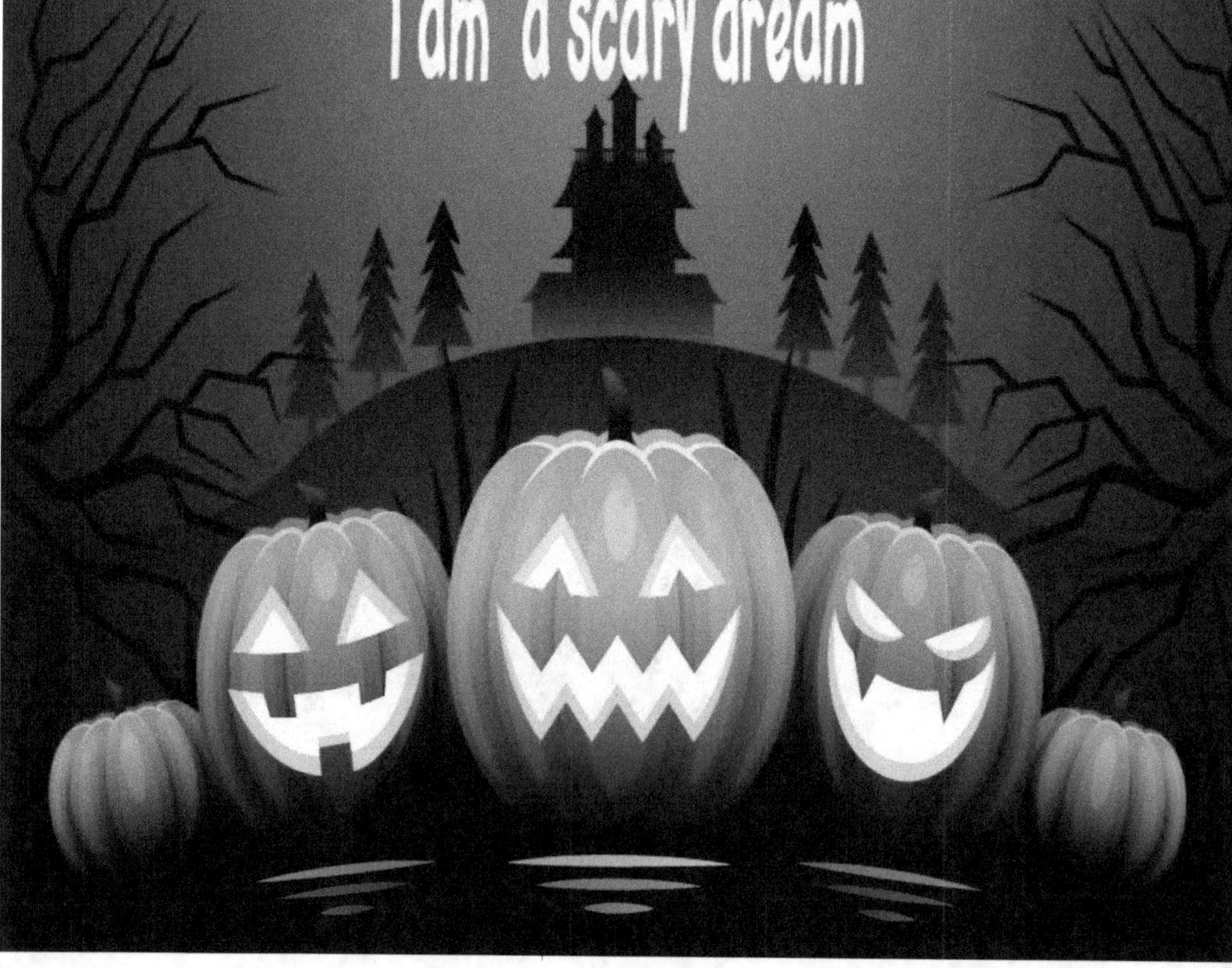
Guess What I Am ?

I Start with a N
I am a scary dream

I am a NIGHTMARE

15/26
Guess What I Am ?
I Start with an O
I live In tree branches

I am a

OWL

16/26
Guess What I Am ?
I Start with a P
I am an orange squash

I am a

PUMPKIN

17/26

Guess What I Am ?

I Start with a Q
I am a royal costume that girls love
to wear.

I am a QUEEN

Guess What I Am ?

I Start with a R
I am a black bird.

I am a

RAVEN

Guess What I Am ?

I Start with a **S**

Day or night my bones are white.

I am a

SKELETON

Guess What I Am ?

20/26

I Start with a T
I am a large stone placed at the
head of a grave.

I am a

TOMBSTONE

Guess What I Am ?

I Start with a U
I am the adjectif that describes the faces

of goblins

I am

UGLY

Guess What I Am ?

I Start with a V

I am a supernatural creature who

beats necks.

22/26

I am a

Guess What I Am ?

I Start with a W
I have magical powers.

I am a

WITCH

24/26
Guess What I Am ?

I Start with an X
I am a photo of bones.

I am an

X-RAY

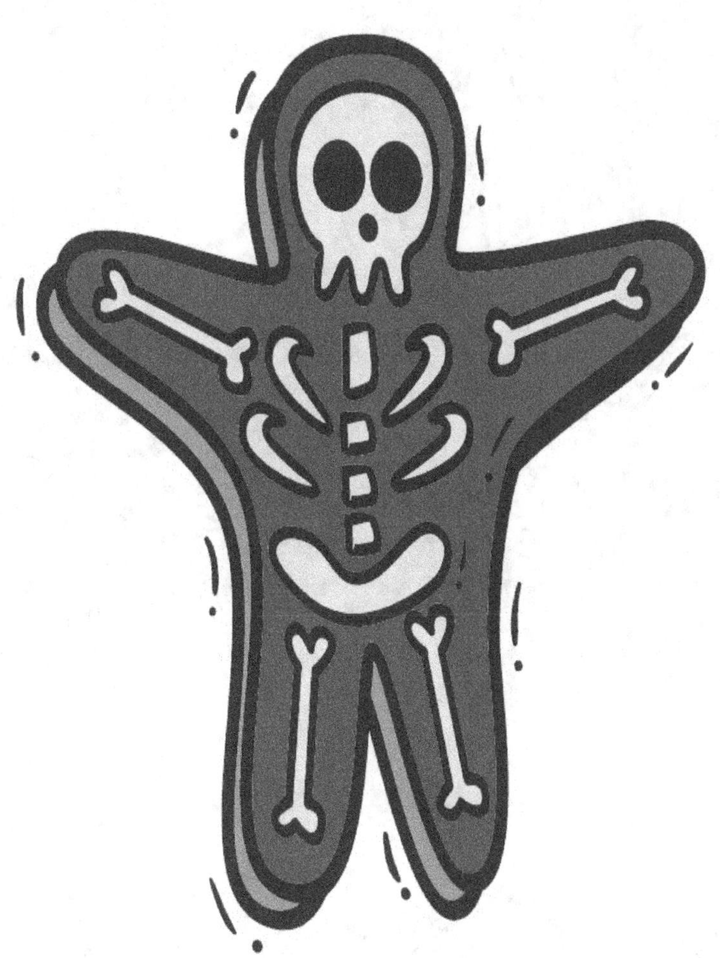

Guess What I Am ?

I am a YELL

25/26
Guess What I Am ?
I Start with a Z
I am an undead creature who
eats human.

I am a
ZOMBIE